Fat, DUMB and LAZY

A simple story for those who seek change
(and even those who don't)

A Not Long Book

Fat, Dumb and Lazy ©2009 by Julie and Brian Long. Printed and bound in the United States of America. All rights reserved. No part of this book may be reproduced or transmitted in any form or by any means, electronic or mechanical, including photocopying, recording, or by any information storage and retrieval system, without written permission from the authors. For information, write to info@fatdumbandlazy.com.

Book design and illustrations by Patricia Tsagaris.
www.pinkhausdesign.com

ISBN 978-0-9843185-0-6

All good things are difficult to achieve; and bad things are very easy to get.
— Confucius

Good Company was successful. It should have been. Its CEO, Mr. Lead, spent a lot of money on things like efficiency consultants, incentive pay, risk transfer mechanisms, ergonomic studies, union contract negotiations, employee retention models and business management strategies.

And all of these things paid off.

Well, maybe not all, but most.

Or at least some.

Which made Good Company good.

Very good.

But not great.

Something, it seemed, 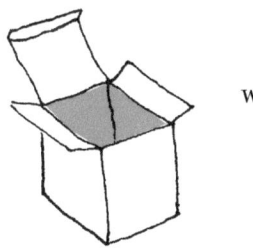 was missing.

Mr. Lead wasn't sure what it was, but he was beginning to wonder if the missing something had to do, not with processes or procedures, but with people.

Were the employees holding Good Company back from being a better company?

Maybe not all of his employees, Mr. Lead reasoned,
but certainly some.
At least a few.
In particular, three:

Fat, DUMB and *LAZY*

Fat, DUMB and LAZY weren't bad people, all in all.

But they weren't good for business.

Actually, they weren't doing themselves much good, either.

Fat wasn't fit. He didn't take care of himself. He was overweight, undernourished and inactive. No one at Good Company said anything because they didn't want to hurt Fat's feelings. And as long as he could do his job,
what business was it of theirs?

But one day Fat fell.

He didn't fall far, but the fall was felt — by him,

and by the company.

Fat missed work.

    A lot of work.

Thirteen times more work than Thin did when he had an accident.

And Fat's medical costs were seven times higher than Thin's. Mr. Lead had to hire a temporary replacement to do Fat's work while he recovered.

And the company's insurance costs increased.

Now, it's hard to say whether Fat would have fallen if he weren't overweight. But, factually speaking, Fat was twice as likely to have an accident on the job.

> A Duke University Medical Center analysis found that obese workers filed twice the number of workers' compensation claims, had seven times higher medical costs from those claims and lost 13 times more days of work from work injury or work illness than did non-obese workers.

Fat, Mr. Lead realized, not only risked his own health. He risked the financial health of Good Company.

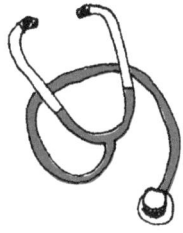

DUMB wasn't stupid.

He just didn't know any better.

He didn't consult the manual.
He didn't pay attention in training.
He didn't follow safety procedures
because he'd never learned them.

All of which wasn't very smart, if you think about it.

Because that meant Dumb made mistakes.

Costly mistakes.

One day Dumb was someplace he shouldn't have been, doing something he shouldn't have been doing. He caused an accident that shouldn't have happened. Even when Dumb was where he was expected to be, doing what was expected of him, his mind wandered ...

Or he got distracted…

And then, sure enough,
something unexpected happened.

The ironic thing was, Dumb thought he knew it all. But of course he didn't. And, as Mr. Lead could've told him,

"It's what you don't know you don't know that'll hurt you."

And your coworkers.
And your company.

Various studies show that up to 80% of accidents are caused by human error, which stems mainly from incorrect or incomplete knowledge.

LAZY wasn't Dumb.

He knew better.

But he did it anyway.

He let his work area slip into disarray.
He skipped wearing protective equipment.
If the right tool wasn't handy he used what was.

Sometimes he did it to make work easier.
Sometimes he did it because he was tired.

Sometimes he simply thought he was skilled enough
    that the rules needn't apply to him.
Lazy had done his job for so long
    that he forgot what a risky environment it was.

It no longer occurred to him to be cautious.

So Lazy took shortcuts.
Lazy cut corners.

And an accident would cut Lazy's career short.
Just like Fat and Dumb, Lazy risked his own health
and livelihood,

                        as well as Good Company's.

            When we're continually in a risky situation,
              it's easy to normalize and forget to be cautious.
Most mountain-climbing accidents happen on the way down from the summit,
                                  not on the way up.

The more Mr. Lead thought about Fat, Dumb and Lazy, the more convinced he became that their behaviors were responsible for keeping Good Company from being great.

If only **Fat,** DUMB and *LAZY* didn't work there.

But Mr. Lead knew it wasn't as simple as that.
Because the more he thought about Fat, Dumb
and Lazy, the more Mr. Lead understood that everyone
behaved like them at times.

Even, he hated to admit, himself.

Somewhere deep inside, in the corner he didn't like to peek in, lurked the truth of what he could change about himself.

Mr. Lead took a deep breath.

Then he took a good, hard look…

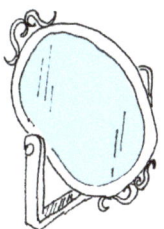

Though Mr. Lead considered himself athletic, in truth it had been years since he'd been physically fit.

> He always took the elevator.
> He never ordered the fish.
> And he drank too much.

While he wasn't fat, with these behaviors it was only a matter of time.

Mr. Lead was smart in his business dealings, but he could think of actions he took in his daily life that reminded him of Dumb. For instance, when he drove to appointments, he would often speed.

Or talk on his phone.
Or both.

He routinely lectured his employees about safety, yet he wasn't practicing what he preached.

According to Virginia Tech Transportation Institute, drivers dialing a cell phone are three times more likely to crash — six times more likely if dialing while driving a truck. Text messaging while driving a heavy vehicle or truck makes the risk of crashing 23 times more likely.

Hardest to admit was something Mr. Lead had in common with Lazy:

>He still smoked.

He knew this was dumb, of course.
But he also knew the real reason he hadn't quit was that it was just too hard. It would take too much effort.

Could he really be so lazy
that he would risk his health?

According to Wellness Councils of America
and The Center for Health Care Economics,
70% of healthcare costs generated in the United States
are attributable to preventable risks and unhealthy choices.

The funny thing was, Mr. Lead now realized, if he could see the poor behaviors of Fat, Dumb and Lazy, his own poor behaviors were probably apparent to others even when he'd refused to notice them.

How could Mr. Lead expect **Fat,** DUMB and *LAZY* to be great when he didn't set a great example?

> The faults of a superior person are like the sun and moon.
> They have their faults, and everyone sees them;
> they change and everyone looks up to them.
> — Confucius

Mr. Lead decided to work on his own behaviors.
And he asked Fat, Dumb and Lazy to do the same.

He asked every employee,

    in every department,

        in every division,

to identify a fat, dumb or lazy behavior of their own.

And change it.

It was going to be hard work for all of them. In fact, they might need to work harder on themselves than they worked at their jobs.

To see the right and not do it is cowardice.
— Confucius

But maybe that's how it should be, Mr. Lead decided. Maybe that was **the missing something** that would take Good Company to great.

Mr. Lead started working harder on himself.

He began exercising regularly. And driving safely.

And using nicotine patches to quit smoking.

He became an inspiration...

Fat worked harder at getting fit.

When Mr. Lead implemented a company wellness program, so any employee who wanted to get healthy received the support they needed, Fat was the first to join.

Dumb worked harder at learning to be safe.

He joined the safety committee and changed the training programs to be more interesting, so more employees would be smart about safety.

And Lazy worked harder at following procedures.

He encouraged others to do the right thing, too,
When Mr. Lead developed a program to highlight good
efforts throughout the company, Lazy won the first award.

Pretty soon, Fat, Dumb and Lazy became known as

Lean, Smart and Industrious.

And so did the company.

Today, Mr. Lead is no longer the CEO of Good Company.

He is the CEO of **Great Company.**

The End.
(But really it's only the beginning...)

CHALLENGE YOURSELF

What is one thing you do that hurts instead of helps you and/or those around you?

_____

What will be your first step toward change?
(Even a journey of a thousand miles begins with a single step.)

_____

When will you begin? (How about today?)

_____

Commit to change by signing your name:

_____

Now share your commitment with someone you care about!

CHALLENGE YOUR COMPANY

Share this story with your coworkers
and ask them to commit
to changing one thing!

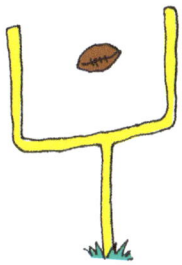

The moment one definitely commits oneself, then Providence moves, too.
All sorts of things occur to help one that would never otherwise have occurred.

— W.H. Murray

I am your constant companion.
I am your greatest helper or heaviest burden.
I will push you onward and upward, or drag you down to failure.
I am completely at your command.
Ninety percent of the things you do
might just as well be turned over to me,
and I will be able to do them quickly and correctly.
I am easily managed,
show me exactly how you want something done
and after a few lessons I will do it automatically.
I am the servant of all great people
and the "alas!" of all failures as well.
I am not a machine,
though I work with all the precision of a machine,
plus the intelligence of a man.
You can run me for profit or run me for ruin
— it makes no difference to me.
Take me, train me, be firm with me
and I will place the world at your feet.
Be easy with me and I will destroy you.
Who am I? I am Habit.

— Anonymous

www.ingramcontent.com/pod-product-compliance
Lightning Source LLC
Chambersburg PA
CBHW041752040426
42446CB00001B/13